DISCARDED
From Nashville Public Library

Property of
Nashville Public Library
615 Church St., Nashville, Tn. 37219

GALAXY OF SUPERSTARS

98°	Faith Hill
Ben Affleck	Lauryn Hill
Jennifer Aniston	Jennifer Lopez
Backstreet Boys	Ricky Martin
Brandy	Ewan McGregor
Garth Brooks	Mike Myers
Mariah Carey	'N Sync
Matt Damon	Gwyneth Paltrow
Cameron Diaz	LeAnn Rimes
Leonardo DiCaprio	Adam Sandler
Céline Dion	Will Smith
Sarah Michelle Gellar	Britney Spears
Tom Hanks	Spice Girls
Hanson	Jonathan Taylor Thomas
Jennifer Love Hewitt	Venus Williams

CHELSEA HOUSE PUBLISHERS

GALAXY OF SUPERSTARS

Will Smith

Meg Greene

CHELSEA HOUSE PUBLISHERS
Philadelphia

Frontis: Always smiling, Will Smith has enjoyed success as both an actor and a singer. An entertainer through and through, there seem to be very few things that Will can't accomplish.

CHELSEA HOUSE PUBLISHERS

Editor in Chief: Sally Cheney
Associate Editor in Chief: Kim Shinners
Production Manager: Pamela Loos
Art Director: Sara Davis

Produced by
21st Century Publishing and Communications, Inc.
New York, New York
http://www.21cpc.com

© 2002 by Chelsea House Publishers, a subsidiary of Haights Cross Communications. All rights reserved. Printed and bound in the United States of America.

The Chelsea House World Wide Web address is
http://www.chelseahouse.com

First Printing

1 3 5 7 9 8 6 4 2

Library of Congress Cataloging-in-Publication Data

Greene, Meg.
   Will Smith / Meg Greene.
      p. cm. — (Galaxy of superstars)
   Includes bibliographical references and index.
   Summary: Explores the personal and professional life of Philadelphia-born Will Smith, a highly successful rap musician, television and film actor whose awards include Grammy and American Music Awards.
   ISBN 0-7910-6469-7 (alk. paper)
   1. Smith, Will, 1968– —Juvenile literature. 2. Actors—United States—Biography—Juvenile literature. 3. Rap musicians—United States—Biography—Juvenile literature. [1. Smith, Will, 1968– . 2. Actors and actresses. 3. Musicians. 4. Rap (Music). 5. African-Americans—Biography.] I. Title. II. Series.

PN2287.S612 G74 2001
791.43'028'092—dc21
  [B]   2001042210

Contents

Chapter 1
"Gettin' Jiggy Wit It"   7

Chapter 2
"In West Philadelphia,   13
Born and Raised"

Chapter 3
"I'm the Rapper"   23

Chapter 4
The Fresh Prince of Bel Air   35

Chapter 5
"Saving the World   45
Every Summer"

Chapter 6
Looking Ahead   53

Chronology   59
Accomplishments   60
Further Reading   62
Index   63

1

"Gettin' Jiggy Wit It"

It was an unbelievable evening. Not once, not twice, but three times Will Smith walked to the podium to accept an award on January 11, 1999. After a four-year absence from the recording studio, Smith's solo effort, *Big Willie Style*, had won big at the American Music Awards.

Will was pleased just to have been nominated; he never dreamed about winning. Following the ceremony, he told the reporters who had gathered backstage that he was not at all sure the album would do well. "It moved from Number 98 (on the *Billboard* charts) to 104. So I was concerned." He need not have worried. "Then Jerry Seinfield started saying 'get jiggy with it.' And that sort of took it off."

Big Willie Style earned four American Music Awards nominations. No one was more surprised than Will when his name was called as the winner three times during the evening at the Shrine Auditorium in Los Angeles. Will won for Best Pop/Rock Album and Favorite Soul/R&B Album. He also took home a statuette for Favorite Soul/R&B Artist. After winning his first of three trophies of the evening, a grateful Will told the crowd of 5,000: "I've been away a while. I'm just glad people are accepting me again making the music." No doubt about it, 1999 was beginning

---

Will Smith accepts his award for Best Rap Solo Performance at the 1999 Grammy Awards.

to look like a great year for Will Smith.

The American Music Awards was only the start. In February, Will took home a Grammy Award for Best Rap Solo Performance for the single "Gettin' Jiggy Wit It," released from *Big Willie Style*. It was the second time he had won the award. Always ready with a joke, Will told the crowd that earlier in the day he had met with his son's teachers at school for a conference. When they told him that his son excelled at math and science, but did poorly at rhyming, Will jokingly replied that his son better study to be a lawyer.

Backstage after the ceremony it was a different story. Will shunned the limelight and managed to detach himself from the crush of media covering the event. He stood quietly with his wife of almost two years, actress Jada Pinkett, and made sure she was comfortable. Later that evening, Jada returned home to be with their son, while Will made the rounds of post-awards parties.

Big Willie Style had been a gamble on Will's part. Concerned about the growing popularity of violent images and language of "gangsta rap," Will decided to return to the studio to record a different kind of rap album. In one interview he explained, "Rap's gone through a sort of dark ages. I think with the loss [deaths] of Biggie [Smalls] and Tupac [Shakur], the rap industry is ready for a change." Will also believed that rap music had moved away from its roots. "The essence of rap was always about partying and having fun. The best rapper was the one that could rock the crowd. How well you shot a gun wasn't part of the criteria."

Will had some reservations about making another album. He had said that he would probably not make any more records after the release of the film *Independence Day* in 1996. Although his successful movie career influenced that decision, there were other considerations. Rap music had begun to change, and Will wasn't sure he wanted to continue his music career.

"I'd almost stopped listening to rap," Will recalled. "Wyclef [Jean] was that person that got me started again. . . . I started coming back in. . . . Then, after 'Pac and Biggie got killed, I felt like, I had to make records. Even if I don't have a hit, I'm putting my energy out there." Will remembered, too, an old promise he had made to his grandmother to keep his music free from the profanity that was becoming the trademark of so many other rap musicians. He also had to think about his son. "I want my son to have a rap record with no profanity–clean and fun," Will declared.

Columbia Records believed the timing was right for Will to make a comeback. "Will Smith is a worldwide superstar," said one Columbia executive. Given Will's previous commercial success, the company fully believed that *Big Willie Style* would be a hit. In November 1997, Columbia launched an aggressive advertising and sales campaign for the album, running both radio and television promotional spots. In addition, there were contests, posters, and billboards announcing the release of *Big Willie Style*. It seemed as if there were reminders everywhere that Will Smith was making music again.

Critics immediately noted a change in Smith's new work. The music and lyrics were more mature and reflected a number of different themes. One radio executive regarded the release of the album as a "second time around for [Will]. I think he's matured and taken his craft and the industry to another level. . . . I think he's one of the few universal hip-hop artists out there." Will had made a successful return to the world of rap.

Will could not have agreed more. "Creatively, this album is more of what I think, what I feel," he said. One of the more popular songs on the album, "Just the Two of Us," was written for his four-year-old son Trey and described Will's thoughts about being a father. While his previous albums had reflected his experiences with DJ Jazzy Jeff, this album showcased Will's life as it was at that moment. As Will himself suggested, "I'm in a different place in my life right now. I've had different life experiences, and I have a whole new outlook on life. I'm rapping off a different POV [point of view]."

With *Big Willie Style,* Will also stepped out from behind his persona "Fresh Prince." The album was without question a Will Smith production. But while this may have been Will's first solo effort, he was hardly alone in the studio. His old partner, "DJ Jazzy Jeff" Townes, worked with him throughout the process and produced three of the album's tracks. Even Will's son, Trey, and wife, Jada, got a chance to sing along. Dropping the nickname that had once identified Will as one of the biggest rap and television stars in the country was no big deal either. "I've been referred to as Fresh Prince for 11 years now," he said in 1997. "It's not that I wanted to change it. I've always just said to people that I'm not a rapper, I'm an entertainer, and Will Smith started to be the way I was more commonly known. I didn't say Fresh Prince is the guy that raps, Will Smith is on TV. [The name change] just kind of happened."

Will Smith displays his Philly pride at the 1998 Grammy Awards. His single, "Men in Black," won the Grammy for Best Rap Solo Performance of the year.

Although Will was firmly back on top in the music world, the film industry also reminded him of his growing popularity at the box office. Not long after his triumphs at the American Music and Grammy Awards, Will learned that he had been named ShoWest's "Actor of the Year" by NATO, an organization of movie exhibitors and theater owners. By 1999, Will had made three movies in a row that grossed more than $100 million.

For the time being, Will Smith was content. At the age of 30, he had made a name for himself as part of a popular rap duo and as a solo recording artist. He had been in a successful television series and was now becoming recognized as a movie star. He had survived a disastrous first marriage and bankruptcy. It had been a long journey from the streets of Philadelphia.

2

"In West Philadelphia, Born and Raised"

The Wynnefield neighborhood, located in West Philadelphia, has been home to many African Americans for the better part of a century. The quiet streets are lined with neat, brick houses. It is, and always has been, a neighborhood of middle-class families determined to do something with their lives.

During the 1960s, many in the neighborhood watched with growing concern as violence exploded in other African-American neighborhoods across the country. Even though many blacks were beginning to see a change for the better in the way they were treated, there was still tension in the United States about race relations. In the midst of the civil rights movement, many African Americans began to challenge the racial discrimination that they encountered every day. It was not easy, but they wanted to believe that the struggle was worth it, if not for themselves then for their children.

Unfortunately for some, rising expectations often bred frustration and anger when change did not take place fast enough. By 1968, many African Americans were taking to the streets in protest against continuing expressions of

---

Will grew up in the Wynnefield section of West Philadelphia. Will's parents believed in hard work and always tried to provide better opportunities for themselves and their children.

racism in the United States. That year was the most tumultuous in an already turbulent decade. Americans suffered two severe blows in quick succession: the assassination of the Reverend Martin Luther King Jr. in April and the assassination of Senator Robert F. Kennedy in June. An entire generation, black as well as white, had viewed King and Kennedy as leaders who would reestablish peace and justice in American society. Now both were gone.

But in Wynnefield, as in other communities around the country, there were those who believed the key to individual success and racial acceptance lay in hard work and pride in one's self. Although many in the neighborhood openly supported the civil rights movement and were critical of many things going on in the country, there were other practical matters to consider, such as succeeding at their jobs, raising their families, and setting good examples for their children. For Willard and Caroline Smith, things were no different. As their son Will described them, the couple were "products of the '60s" who were committed to social change and better opportunities for themselves, but more importantly, for their children.

For Willard Smith Sr. these ideals became even more important as his family grew. On September 25, 1968, at Children's Hospital, Caroline had just given birth to their second child and first son, Willard "Will" C. Smith Jr. The Smiths were already the parents of a daughter, Pamela, born five years earlier. Now there was a son to carry on the family name. Not more than three years later, the Smiths made two more additions to the family, with twins Harry and Ellen. That many children made the little brick house more crowded and noisy but also happy and full of life.

Will's father was one of the few men in the neighborhood to own his own business. His company, Arcac, designed and installed commercial refrigeration equipment. Will's mother worked, too, as an administrator at the board of education. Despite their busy schedules, both parents found time to spend with their children, whether it was helping them with their homework, playing a game, or reading aloud. Will's particular favorites were the Dr. Seuss books with their clever rhymes and nonsensical stories. He, in fact, credits the stories with having a real influence on the way he would react to hip-hop so many years later: "If you listen to them a certain way, books like *Green Eggs and Ham* and *Hop on Pop* sound a lot like hip-hop." On another occasion Will declared, "Words and rhymes got me going." Will also liked to make up stories of his own in which he was a superhero with amazing powers.

What Will remembers most about his early years is the love and attention his parents devoted to their children. As he told one interviewer, "We were all made to feel special." To another interviewer he was even more clear about his feelings toward his mother and father: "The only people I continue to idolize are my parents. They taught me clearly the difference between right and wrong, and that when you make a mistake you must be honest with yourself about it."

Will's mother remembers her son's precocious personality. "He could talk before he could walk," she once commented. And after Will found his voice, there was no shutting him up. Along with his quick mastery of language,

Will credits his parents, Caroline and Willard Smith Sr., with giving him a loving and supportive upbringing. He recalls, "They taught me clearly the difference between right and wrong."

though, Will discovered that he was good at making people laugh. Will doesn't take all the credit. He admits, "I was blessed with a really, really funny family. Dinnertime was like a nightly laugh riot."

Life also had its serious moments in the Smith household. Will's father was in charge of discipline, something he took very seriously. Early on, he believed it was important for his children to understand the difference between right and wrong and to recognize that there were limits to their freedom. "My father was the man with all the answers," Will admitted. "He did his shaping by taking little chunks out of your behind."

Although Willard Sr. was tough, he was neither bullying nor cruel. "He'd get this look," Will once recalled, "that said, 'One more step, Will, and it'll get ugly.'" Even after he was punished, Will still found it possible to joke. His brother, Harry, remembered that Will often was punished first because he was the older brother. Then afterward, Will would go around a corner and make faces that made his younger brother and sister burst out laughing. Unfortunately, his behavior meant the punishments tended to get a little stiffer. Yet, because of the discipline his father imposed, Will has always looked to his father as a steadying and positive influence in his life.

There was yet another person in Will's life who had a tremendous influence on him. His maternal grandmother, Helen Bright, encouraged Will in his musical and comic interests early on. All of the Smith children loved music and were urged to learn to play a musical instrument and sing. Will decided to learn the piano because it was his mother's favorite instrument. That did not stop him from trying out his brother's and sisters' instruments, though, as Will was drawn to anything musical.

With his grandmother's help, Will made his first venture into acting. Mrs. Bright was very active in her church, Resurrection Baptist. There, she was in charge of everything from holiday plays to church programs to Easter egg hunts. Will made his stage debut in one of the holiday plays staged at the church. As much as he enjoyed the attention he received from performing in front of an audience, Will's idea of an ideal career was not that of an actor or even of a musician. Will longed to become an astronaut!

When it came to the children's education, Will's mother was in charge. Even though she worked for the local school system, Caroline Smith wanted the best for her children. As a result, Will and his brother and sisters attended the local Catholic school, Our Lady of Lourdes. For the next nine years, Will worked hard at school. He earned a reputation as a good student who excelled at math and science. Will's other favorite subject, though, was English, in which his writing, especially his poetry, earned high praise from teachers and students alike.

Not surprisingly, Will also came to be known as the class clown. He loved to tell jokes and funny stories. His way with words earned him many friends who never tired of his antics. As he later explained it: "It's always been fun for me to tell a story and make people laugh. I've always been a show-off, and uncomfortable when people weren't looking at me."

Will's physical appearance was cause for comment, too. Will described his early "look" to one interviewer stating, "When I was little, everybody always told me I looked like Alfred E. Newman, the weird guy on the cover of *Mad Magazine*. I always had that square-looking fade hairdo, and I liked it, even though it made my ears stick out. One guy once told me I looked like a car with the doors open."

In 1981, when Will was 13 years old, the Smith household was rocked by a shocking and sad announcement. Will's parents told the children that they were getting a divorce. As much as they loved their children, Will's mother and

"IN WEST PHILADELPHIA, BORN AND RAISED"

Will attended Our Lady of Lourdes Catholic grade school in Philadelphia. Will's favorite subject was English, and he excelled at math and science.

father could no longer stay together. They had kept the problems in their marriage a secret for a long time, but now they felt it was time to separate for good. For 13-year-old Will, the news was a bombshell.

The Smiths decided that Will, Harry, and Ellen would stay with their mother. Will's older sister, Pamela, was at college and no longer living at home. Despite his absence from the house, Willard remained a strong presence in his son's life, continuing to take an active role in all of his children's upbringing and welfare.

Willard Smith often taught lessons by example and experience. Both of Will's parents, for instance, knew that for a teenager seeking to be popular, the temptation to try drugs was almost overwhelming. Instead of simply talking to Will

Will's parents taught their children to believe in themselves. They are the only people he continues to idolize to this day.

about the perils of drug abuse, his father decided to show him the kind of trouble drugs could cause. He drove Will to the roughest part of Philadelphia. From his car window Will saw people sleeping in the doorways of abandoned buildings and drug addicts standing on street corners hoping to make a score. Will remembered the experience vividly: "He pointed to the bums sleeping in the doorways and said, 'This is what people look like when they do drugs.'" Willard Sr. made his point. His son never did drugs.

Will remembers this time in his life as being filled with love and support from both his parents, despite their divorce. "We never felt like our parents didn't love us," Will recalled. "No matter how difficult things got or how angry someone may have gotten, no matter what happened . . . we always felt we had somewhere to go." Reinforcing the self-esteem that came with his parents' love was the way in which the Smiths taught their children to believe in themselves. One lesson Will remembers particularly well. His father told Will and his brother Harry to rebuild a brick wall that was tumbling down. The two boys spent the next several months demolishing the wall so that they could begin the long, slow, difficult process of rebuilding it. When they finally finished, Will Sr. told them, "Now don't ever tell me that you can't do something." It was one of the best pieces of advice Will ever received. Will said that whenever he was filled with doubts or fears about trying something new, "I think about that wall, and tell myself, one brick at a time."

His parents' divorce made little impact on Will's schoolwork and his other activities. By the time he was a teenager, Will was busy with school, working at his father's shop after school, or just hanging out with friends. But by 1981, Will had found something else to occupy much of his time and imagination: rap music.

3

"I'm the Rapper"

Will Smith loved music. From the time he was 10 years old, he had spent countless hours listening to all kinds of music on the stereo system his father bought for him. He was especially partial to funk, one of the popular musical styles of the 1970s. Then, in 1979, Will heard a kind of music unlike any other he had ever experienced. A song titled "Rapper's Delight" came on the radio. While the song had the funky rhythms that Will admired, he was most impressed by the vocalist who talked over the music, making clever rhymes and cracking jokes. Will couldn't believe his ears. From that moment he was hooked.

Will didn't know yet that the new sound hitting the airwaves across the United States was called "rap." In its early years, rap was mostly street music played at parties and clubs in such large cities as New York and Los Angeles. The style had emerged from the "toasters," Jamaican musicians who took existing records and, by manipulating them on turntables, recycled "old" music into something completely new and different. Although growing in popularity during the late 1970s, rap still had a limited audience, restricted largely to the African-American community.

Will got his big break in music when he met local Philly disc jockey DJ Jazzy Jeff in 1985. Soon they were recording songs together and planning to release an album.

"Rapper's Delight" was among the first attempts to expose a larger audience to rap. Seemingly overnight, rap, or hip-hop as it soon came to be known, was heard everywhere. Hip-hop was more than a new musical style. It also generated something of a social revolution among young blacks. For African-American kids throughout the country, hip-hop was about a way of living. In time, the music began to evolve from the feel-good and funny party music to more serious songs, many of which reflected social concerns such as poverty, violence, drug abuse, and racism. Will described the impact that hip-hop had on his musical education and his social consciousness. He said, "When you grow up in any urban area, particularly a black area, you can't escape it. Rap is the urban music. Everybody in the street is a rapper, or a DJ, or a beat box. Hip-hop is a culture. It's not just music, it's a way of life."

Will quickly immersed himself in hip-hop. Given his way with words and his sense of humor, Will quickly established himself as one of the hottest and youngest rappers in the Philadelphia area. He was a popular fixture at many local block parties where rappers got together to perform. As Will recalls, "My reputation came from beating other rappers in street challenges. I never lost a street battle."

Unlike other rappers though, Will quickly discarded the profanity that was such an integral part of most hip-hop songs. In an interview Will explained why he decided not to use foul language in his raps: "In the beginning, following the fashion of the day, my raps had a small amount of profanity. I'll never forget what my grandmother said when she read them: 'He who is truly articulate shuns profanity.' " It was a turning point for Will: "Man, I didn't even know what 'articulate' meant, but I knew I wanted my grandmother's approval, just as I wanted my parents' approval."

By this time, Will had left Our Lady of Lourdes for Overbrook High School. Where once Will had stood out, he was now just one of many faces in the crowd. To get himself noticed, Will fell back on his role as class clown. His sense of humor, combined with his growing reputation as one of the city's best rappers, soon made Will many friends.

Will continued to study, though not with quite the same zeal as he had displayed at Our Lady of Lourdes. "I got the grades mainly to please my parents," he admitted once. "I didn't think I'd ever use what I learned." He still joked around in class, but also managed to take in what was being taught. When asked to describe himself in high school, Will was to the point: "I was just silly all the time. People I went to school with probably remember me as a jackass." It was also in high school that Will earned a new nickname, Prince Charming, for his ability to talk himself out of sticky situations in a creative and entertaining fashion.

Although Will was active in various school groups, such as the chess club and the Motivation Program aimed at college-bound students, he spent most of his time refining his music. Whereas he had once dreamed of conquering space, he now dreamed of conquering the music industry. During this period, Will had put together an act with a friend, Clarence "Clate" Holmes, who was known for his ability to get rhythmic sounds out of just about any part of his body. By now, Will had been perfecting his raps and believed it was time to take a chance on his abilities.

He and Holmes contacted a local record company, Word Up, which was making a name for itself in hip-hop music. Will spoke with the label's producer, Dana Goodman, about his music. Goodman was more than happy to listen to what the two had to offer. Although Goodman was impressed with the duo's abilities, he did not think that they had enough material to do an album. He told the boys to come back when they had more songs. For Will that was enough encouragement to convince him that he was moving in the right direction.

Will, of course, could not devote all of his time to music. He had other responsibilities to consider, school being chief among them. Both his parents and his teachers pushed Will to take his studies more seriously, reminding him that he needed something to fall back on in case he did not succeed with his music. He continued to make above-average grades, but it was clear his heart was no longer in his schoolwork. Music was becoming the focus of his life.

Will began to consider the possibility that his future was in a musical career. He now clearly thought of himself as a professional and so charged a fee to perform at parties. By this time, too, his style of rapping had become a distinctive blend of subtle humor and skillful wordplay that almost everyone enjoyed.

For a while Will was content to enjoy his new celebrity and build a music career. Then in 1986 everything changed. While attending a party in his neighborhood, Will met a local disc jockey named Jeff Townes. Known as "DJ Jazzy Jeff," Townes was four years older than Will and had been one of the top hip-hop DJs in Philadelphia for several years. Jeff had heard of Will but had never met him. At the party they talked for the first time. Townes described their meeting:

> I was the best DJ in Philadelphia and I had heard of Will. . . . But when I played that party on Will's block, naturally he was there. He asked if he could rap for a while and I said yes. He started rapping and I started cutting, and it was like natural chemistry. He flowed with what I did and I flowed exactly with what he did and we knew it. We just clicked the whole night long. The chemistry between us was so good.

In 1986, Will took the name Fresh Prince and formed a rap duo with DJ Jazzy Jeff. They released their first album, *Rock the House*, the following year.

Before long, Will and Jeff were working parties and clubs together. The more time they spent with each other, the better friends they became. In fact, the two were very similar. Jeff had grown up not far from Wynnefield and had a middle-class upbringing comparable to Will's. Like Will, Jeff fell in love with hip-hop the first time he heard it, and from then on devoted countless hours to perfecting his craft.

Will and Jeff's skills were complementary. Will's attraction to rap was primarily the words. For Jeff, it was the sound and the rhythm. Jeff loved the way a DJ could rearrange the music that already existed into a totally different song. By the age of 10, Jeff was already hard at work to become a first-rate DJ. As a teenager, Jeff experimented with all kinds of material on his own home recording equipment, which he set up in the basement of his parents' house. Unlike other DJs who relied on the heavy funk beats, Jeff looked elsewhere for inspiration. His use of jazz, the music he loved more than any other, became his signature.

After school and on weekends, Will and Jeff got together to make music. Along with Will's partner, Clate Holmes, they began recording original songs. First, the boys discussed what they wanted to say, drawing on their own experiences as inspiration. Then the actual work on the song began. Will was in charge of the lyrics; Jeff wrote the music.

Instead of reflecting the gritty edge of the urban ghetto, Will, Jeff, and Clate sang about growing up, dating girls from school, playing video games, dealing with parents, and going to parties and the movies. These were perhaps not subjects common to hip-hop, but they were things to which both black and white kids could relate.

Will's growing enthusiasm for music began to put a strain on his time. He began devoting less of himself to his studies. His teachers told his parents that although Will was clearly capable of doing college-level work, he was not motivated, and, as a result, was just getting by. Dismayed, Will's parents gave him an ultimatum. School came first, music second. If music interfered with doing well in high school, the music would have to go.

Will learned a hard lesson about what happens when one puts fun before responsibility. One weekend Will's father told him that he needed help with a big job at a local delicatessen. He wanted Will ready to go work on Saturday morning at 6 A.M. Unfortunately, Will had performed at a party the night before and did not arrive home until 15 minutes before he was supposed to leave to help his father. Once they had arrived at the deli, Will and his father found that the basement in which they were to work was flooded. Will held the flashlight while his father did the actual work. Tired, Will began to nod off and dropped the flashlight into the water.

The next thing Will knew, his father was screaming. Will miraculously found the flashlight in the water and shined it in the direction from which his father's voice had come. The sight was unforgettable. His father's hair was standing on end, and his fingertips were smoking. Will's father was so angry that he punched his son hard in the chest. Will complained that he felt the blow every day for the next 10 years, but the incident made him agree to get more serious about school and life.

In 1986, Will reached his senior year of high school. He took his SAT exams, did well, and applied to a number of colleges. While he was thinking about applying to the prestigious Massachusetts Institute of Technology (MIT), Will found out that he had been accepted to the Milwaukee School of Engineering. He was pleased, but he had to admit to himself that he was not really interested in going to college; he wanted to make music.

When Will wasn't studying or filling out college applications, he was at Jeff's house. While the music was evolving, the two decided they needed a new name to go with their new sound. Jeff continued to use his nickname DJ Jazzy Jeff, but Will was stuck. He liked the nickname given to him at school, but somehow Prince Charming did not seem the best name for a rapper. In the end, Will settled on Prince and added the word "fresh." For Will, "'Fresh' was *the* word. It was street talk for cool, the best." The Fresh Prince was born.

Remembering Dana Goodman's open invitation to submit more material when they had some, Will and Jeff made demo tapes of their songs and sent them to Goodman. The producer was so pleased with what he heard that he hastened to sign the boys to a recording contract. For Will, not yet out of high school, this turn of events was almost unbelievable. Not long afterward, the pair's first single, "Girls Ain't Nothing But Trouble," was released in 1986.

The song was a hit. Soon it received play not only in Philadelphia but all over the country. With a classic pop theme exploring the uncertainties of teen romance, many teens, black and white, saw "Girls Ain't Nothing But Trouble," as *their* song. The single sold more than 100,000 copies in the United States alone and became a Top 20 hit in England. As a result of their success, Will and Jeff moved to a better-known record label, Jive Records, to cut their first album and begin to plan a concert tour.

In early 1987, Jeff and Will's *Rock the House* was released. The album was unlike any other rap album then on the market. Instead of the hard, political edge that groups like Public Enemy incorporated into their music, Will and Jeff's first effort had more of an upbeat, feel-good sound. The two did not pretend that they were savvy, streetwise ghetto youths. That had simply not been part of their experience. Instead, they stuck to what they knew best, teen experiences that almost everybody, regardless of their background, could relate to. The record was a runaway best-seller, selling over 600,000 copies and earning a gold record (for sales exceeding 500,000 albums). For two youngsters from Philly, the success was overwhelming.

In the meantime, Will had made a hard decision. He told his parents that he wanted to pursue a career in music; his early success convinced him

that he could do so. A music career, though, meant postponing college. Will's parents were not pleased, but they supported their son's decision. Yet, they did impose a few conditions. Will's father told him to "take a year. If it works, God bless you. If it doesn't, you'll go to college." Will's mother was more apprehensive. He explained in an interview, "My mother told all the schools I got into to hold the dorm room, just hoping I'd change my mind." But Will's mind was made up. He was going to make his mark with his music.

In the next year, Will and Jeff began work on their second album and went on tour with the Def Jam Rap Extravaganza, which featured such noted hip-hop artists as LL Cool J and Public Enemy. In 1988 they released their second album, *He's the DJ, I'm the Rapper*, on Jive Records. A double-album, the set featured the hit "Parents Just Don't Understand." The single went platinum, which meant that it sold more than 1 million copies. The story of a teen going shopping

After the success of their first album, DJ Jazzy Jeff and the Fresh Prince were becoming the top rappers in the music industry. In 1998, the rap duo's single, "Parents Just Don't Understand," went platinum.

with his mother had teenagers all over America laughing and nodding their heads in agreement. Another song, "Nightmare on My Street," followed and received an equally enthusiastic response. The album itself went triple platinum with more than 3 million copies sold. The success of the album, phenomenal in itself, was even more so because most recording executives considered hip-hop a musical style of interest only to blacks. Jive Records did not make much of an effort to market the album to a white audience.

But in large part it was Will and Jeff's music that helped to pull hip-hop into the mainstream. In fact, most of the kids who bought *He's the DJ, I'm the Rapper* were not black. Instead they were white teenagers who could relate to the middle-class dreams, frustrations, and experiences of Jazzy Jeff and the Fresh Prince. Without meaning to, they had become the first crossover hip-hop artists.

Their music, however, didn't escape criticism. Many rap artists accused the two of not being black enough and of creating music simply for white consumption. Will and Jeff were hurt and angry about this criticism. Will addressed the criticisms in an interview:

> Our music is black music. Our families are black; we come from black backgrounds. . . . I don't think anyone can dictate what's black and what's not black. . . . We're trying to show the world, and black kids, that you can dress nicely and still be considered black.

Will and Jeff also faced the charge that their music was not authentic because they shunned the use of profanity. Again, Will met the critics head-on, declaring, "I would never do anything that my mother couldn't turn on her radio and listen to. I would never do anything to offend my family." Will had not forgotten his grandmother's wise words on using profanity.

Despite the criticism, Jeff and Will found the music industry more than willing to recognize their contributions and honor their accomplishments. In 1989 the two were nominated for Best Rap Album and Best Rap Artist at the annual American Music Awards, winning in both categories. A month later, they were nominated for a Grammy Award in the newly created rap category for the song "Parents Just Don't Understand."

Upon learning that they won the award, Jeff and Will refused to attend the ceremony because the award was to be given at a nontelevised ceremony along with technical awards. By not showing up to receive the award, Jeff and Will made a statement about the artistic value and importance of rap music. From that point on, the award for rap music was made a part of the televised portion of the Grammys. To their credit, the duo was helping the music industry seriously think of rap as an influential music style.

At the end of the 1980s, Jeff and Will again returned to the studio to begin work on their third album. Unfortunately, *And in This Corner* was not the blockbuster its predecessors had been, or what Will had hoped for. Sales were respectable, but there was no break-out single. The album did earn another Grammy nomination. Yet, that recognition could not conceal that something had changed. At age 18 Will Smith had it all: success, fame, and money. He was on top of the music world, but he already seemed to be on the way down. By 1990 the decline was apparent, as Will found himself in the midst of a personal and professional crisis. What had gone wrong?

4

THE FRESH PRINCE OF BEL AIR

"There's nothing more sobering than having six cars and a mansion one day and you can't even buy gas for the cars the next," recalls Will. Almost overnight, Will had gone from being a multimillionaire with cars, houses, jewelry, and money to being completely broke. Worse, in 1990 he owed the Internal Revenue Service more than $1 million! Will was at a loss to explain how his life had crumbled so completely. This wasn't supposed to be happening.

When he and Jeff first started to become successful, Will had insisted that they do everything with style. Since they had the money, the sky was the limit. Both Will and Jeff started living the life of rock stars, complete with limousines, private shopping sprees at exclusive stores, meals at the best restaurants, the fastest cars, and the biggest homes. Will was particularly fond of jewelry, spending thousands on gold watches, rings, and diamond necklaces. He spent money as fast, and sometimes faster, than he earned it. Will was out of control, and no one could restrain him. The checks came in his name and went into his bank account. Will now had to look for things to spend his money on, since he had gotten just about everything he ever wanted. At one point, Will

---

Will Smith made his name in acting with the premiere of his new TV sitcom, *The Fresh Prince of Bel Air*. The show remained on NBC's primetime schedule for six seasons.

spent more than $800,000 in one year.

Although Will insisted that success had not changed him, his parents thought otherwise. They had worked hard to raise Will right. Seeing him throw his money away saddened them at first. Then it made them angry. Once when Will told his father that he owned six cars, his father asked him, "Why do you need six cars when you only have one butt?" As Will later admitted, "He saw me blowing money that could allow me to set myself up for the rest of my life."

Despite the new cars, new clothes, and new friends, Will finally had to admit to himself that something was missing from his life. He began to sense that it was no longer fun to spend money. Will also had to face certain other unpleasant realities as well. Despite the money and the fame, Will, as a young black man, had to explain how he had acquired his cars during random stops by the police. The fancy cars, expensive jewelry, and fine clothes raised suspicions that Will was involved in criminal activity.

In addition, with the disappointing sales from their third album, *And in This Corner*, Will and Jeff were no longer on the cutting edge of rap music. They were being left behind by newer rap artists. The worst was yet to come. Will and Jeff learned that they owed about $10 million in back taxes on their earnings. Without a business manager, Will and Jeff had simply neglected to pay taxes, and they did not now have the money to meet their financial obligations. For the first time in his life, Will was in serious trouble.

He wondered what to do. He knew, of course, that he could count on the support of his family and his real friends. His new "friends" deserted him once the money disappeared. To get back on his feet and start to make sense of his life, Will

The Fresh Prince of Bel Air

After the amazing success of their first two albums, DJ Jazzy Jeff and the Fresh Prince experienced financial trouble with disappointing sales from their third album, *And in This Corner*.

sold off his cars, put his mansion on the market, and moved back to his mother's house. He had hoped that brisk sales of the recent album would enable him to pay off his remaining debts, but it was not to be. He was bankrupt and in debt, and there seemed no way out of the predicament.

Will was still at a loss about how to solve his financial problems when, in late 1989, he flew to California to appear on a television anniversary special honoring Disneyland. While there, he was invited to appear on the popular *Arsenio Hall Show*. After he'd finished taping, Will left to attend a Los Angeles Lakers basketball game.

Not knowing the way to the Great Western Forum, where the Lakers played, Will stopped a young man in the parking lot to ask for directions. It was a fateful meeting, for Will could not have realized that in asking directions to the stadium he was also about to change the direction of his whole life.

The young man whom Will had stopped was Benny Medina, an African-American record producer and vice president in charge of black music at Warner Brothers Records. The two men knew each other slightly, having met once before. Medina had long been at work on an idea for a television show about African Americans—a show based on Medina's own life.

Medina had grown up in an East Los Angeles ghetto. After his mother died, he was shuttled to various youth shelters but had no permanent home. When he was a teenager, Medina at last escaped his nomadic life in rough neighborhoods when a Jewish family living in Beverly Hills adopted him. After struggling to overcome his initial culture shock, Medina blossomed in his new surroundings. Looking back on his experience, Medina believed they might provide the basis for an interesting sitcom that would appeal to both black and white audiences.

For Will Smith, the chance encounter with Benny Medina could not have come along at a better time. Will had been thinking about pursuing an acting career but hadn't had the opportunity to do so. Medina gave Will the chance he'd been waiting for, and Will immediately committed himself to the project. Medina then took the idea to Quincy Jones, an influential musician and producer. By early 1990, Jones had signed on as executive producer of the proposed program. Jones took Medina to the offices of NBC to outline his idea to programming executives. In 10 minutes, Benny Medina described how "a streetwise kid moves in with a rich black family suffering from cultural denial." Medina then explained his own background to show that, in fact, the scenario was realistic. Brandon Tartikoff, then director of NBC's entertainment division, listened to Medina's pitch. When Medina had finished, Tartikoff stood up and said, "Hmm, cute life." Medina didn't know how to interpret the remark, until the next day when NBC agreed to produce the show.

Quincy Jones invited executives from NBC to his home to watch Will audition for the lead role. The reaction to Will's performance was electric. "There were no beads of sweat," said Warren Littlefield, NBC's entertainment president. "Will read from a script and nailed it. I sat there thinking 'Whoa! Just bottle this guy!'" As for Will, landing the role was his salvation. "I was blessed when I got the show," he told one interviewer. "And stone broke." But the NBC programmers were confident about their new show and their new star. Even before the program aired, they boasted that Will would be as big as Eddie Murphy, another popular black comedian who got his start at NBC. Will's expectations were more modest and, perhaps, more realistic. "Give me four or five years, and let me practice. I am nowhere near Eddie Murphy," he admitted to *People* magazine in 1990.

On September 10, 1990, *The Fresh Prince of Bel Air* debuted on NBC. In the beginning, the show held its own, gradually gaining momentum and winning over more viewers. Medina's original premise remained intact. Will played a rapper from West Philadelphia whose mother sends him to live with relatives in Bel Air, California, to

Quincy Jones, a famous producer, helped get Will's acting career off the ground by signing on as executive producer for his show. They had no trouble convincing NBC *The Fresh Prince of Bel Air* would be a hit.

escape mounting gang violence. Will injected a lot of his own experiences and personality into his character, who also happened to be named Will. Throughout its six-year run, *The Fresh Prince of Bel Air* consistently presented shows filled with gentle humor. The show also tried to go beyond the ordinary sitcom formula to address sensitive and controversial social issues such as racism and what Will called "black on black prejudice." He told one interviewer, "There is a full, wide spectrum of black people. And everyone is represented on the show. We're showing something that's never been shown on television."

Despite the growing popularity of *Fresh Prince*, the first two seasons were excruciating for Will. When asked to evaluate his first few performances, Will admits he was terrible. He often forgot his stage directions and mouthed the other actors' lines so he would not miss his own cues. His cast members agreed. "I couldn't believe what a bad actor he was," said costar

Tatyana Ali, who played Will's young cousin Ashley Banks on the show. "I'd do a scene with him and he would mouth my words while I was doing my lines."

Will's inexperience notwithstanding, the audience took his character into their hearts. Viewers never knew what to expect from Will. His snappy one-liners and the sometimes outrageous clothing that he wore became the trademarks of his character that viewers found endearing. "By the third season," Will remembers, "I had come into my own" as an actor, showing such a polish and ease before the cameras that it was hard to believe he had ever been afraid of performing.

Still, the show had its share of critics. Many of Will's peers in the hip-hop world thought the show gave a false impression of African-American life. The criticism reached such a crescendo that Will felt compelled to respond. "I have a different way of expressing myself. I like blending a message with comedy so it's subtle. I want people to enjoy themselves, and then be left with something subliminally." He added, "What I'm happiest about is that I can be a role model and give people something to think about. It's important to have a black show that's positive." Some NBC executives, by contrast, became concerned that the audience for a show featuring a hip-hop singer might dwindle following the controversies that arose about the violent and vulgar lyrics of much rap music and the altercations with the law in which rap groups such as 2 Live Crew had been involved.

Will also answered the critics in another, more direct way. In 1991 he and Jeff returned to the studio to record their fourth album. In the midst of working on a weekly television show, Will had not lost touch with his musical roots. As he explained, "I am a rapper. I will *always* be a rapper."

Musically, Jeff and Will picked up where they had left off. The result was *Homebase*, released in 1991. While hip-hop in general had become much more sinister, dominated by songs that glorified guns, racism, and violence, Will and Jeff stayed with the positive music for which they were noted. Of all the tracks, "Summertime" proved to be the breakout hit. Released as a single with an enjoyable video that received a good deal of air play, the song quickly became the summer anthem for teenagers throughout the United States. But the greatest honor of all came in February 1992 when the Fresh Prince and DJ Jazzy Jeff received their second Grammy Award, this time for Best Rap Performance by a Duo or Group for "Summertime." It also was a not-so-subtle reminder to the music industry that Will was back and better than ever.

Will and Jeff were also honored in 1992 with an NAACP Image Award as Outstanding Rap Artists, while *The Fresh Prince of Bel Air* won an award for Best Comedy Series. Will was nominated for a Golden Globe Award for Best Performance by an Actor in a Television Series. The recognition was flattering but, more important, it showed Will just how far he had come from those early, uncomfortable days on the set, to say nothing of the journey he had made since that fateful night when he had stopped to ask for directions in a Los Angeles parking lot.

Will was pleased with his success. He also seemed to have put his personal life in order. Yet, Will was not satisfied, and he began to think about the future. What would he do next? He had come a long way. Where would he

The *Fresh Prince of Bel Air* premiered on September 10, 1990. Will's warm personality and charisma made the show an immediate hit with viewers.

go from here? Will remained committed to his music and to the television series. He had learned the hard way, though, that nothing lasts forever. His recording contract called for one more album. Both he and Jeff wanted to continue making music, but, realizing that they were no longer on the cutting edge of rap as they once had been, they had reached a crossroads in their careers. The television series did better every season, but that, too, would one day run its course. As Will contemplated his future, he came to see that there was only one logical career choice for him to make: He would try to land a film role.

5

"Saving the World Every Summer"

By 1991 things were definitely going well for Will. He was 23 years old and the star of a hit television series, his latest album was doing brisk business, and, most important, he paid off his huge tax bill. He was eager to grow as an actor and to take on more serious and demanding roles. A small part in the obscure 1986 film *The Imagemaker* gave Will a taste of what it was like to act in the movies. Now he was ready to take on greater challenges.

The *Imagemaker* aside, Will's first real opportunity to act in a movie came in 1992 when he accepted the role of the disabled, homeless Manny in the film *Where the Day Takes You*. The plot, which focused on a group of homeless teens, was often disturbing and sad. Although the movie was not a big hit, Will demonstrated that he could handle a dramatic role.

To gain additional experience, Will accepted a smaller role in the 1993 comedy *Made in America*, in which he played opposite two of Hollywood's hottest comic actors, Whoopi Goldberg and Ted Danson. The movie was only moderately successful, but again Will captured the attention of the producers and director.

In between acting in films and on television, Will found time to go back into the studio with Jeff to make their 1993

The blockbuster hit *Independence Day* transformed Will into a major movie star. He became one of the hottest actors in Hollywood.

album *Code Red*. Compared to their earlier efforts, the record was a commercial failure. Will did the album to honor his contractual obligations, which then freed him to pursue his acting career in earnest. In some ways, Will felt that the time had come to stand back from music. Hip-hop was clearly changing, but for Will there were other considerations, too. He had conquered the music industry and shown what he could do. Along with Jeff, he had helped to bring hip-hop further into the mainstream. Together they had been honored for their contributions, and Will felt that now was the time to move on.

Later in 1993, Will was offered his biggest and most challenging role to date: that of a young, homosexual con man who moves in with a wealthy white family and takes advantage of their hospitality. As Will told one interviewer: "If you lined up one hundred films, this would be the last one that people would expect me to do."

Will was right. The 1994 movie, *Six Degrees of Separation*, explored a number of controversial issues such as racism, class differences, and homosexuality. Will's role was by far the most difficult and demanding that he had yet attempted in his fledgling movie career. Will believed that if the audience could accept him as a conniving and somewhat unattractive character, instead of as the funny and appealing character he played on television, then he would know that he had made progress as an actor.

The script for *Six Degrees of Separation* also appealed to Will, who could relate to some of the film's themes. "I meet people every day [to whom] I would be just another nigger if I didn't have a TV show. It's like, 'Well, I wouldn't let just any black guy into my house. But Will Smith, he's okay. He's a good black guy.' That's just something you learn to deal with."

At first, the film's executive producers did not want Will for the part, thinking the audience would not find him credible or would not enjoy watching the beloved Fresh Prince playing a con man who takes advantage of people. Their reluctance, however, did not stop Will from auditioning for the role. On the contrary, their opposition to him getting the part motivated him. "My drive was the fact that they didn't want me," he said. "They didn't think I could do it. They thought I was the *worst* choice you could have for the role." Even after Will demonstrated that he could handle the complex part, the producers were still not convinced. It was only after one of the film's financial backers, who had known Will from an earlier film, stated that he would withdraw funding for *Six Degrees of Separation* if Will were not given the role, that the executive producers backed down and gave Will the role.

In 1994, Will landed a role in the movie *Six Degrees of Separation*. It was one of his most challenging roles in his early days as an actor.

At the insistence of the producers and the director, Will, for the next three months, worked intensively with dialect and acting coaches to learn how to speak like his character, Paul, and to sharpen his general acting skills. Will was happy to cooperate. He knew by now that learning how best to utilize his acting talent took time, patience, and effort. He was also looking beyond *Six Degrees of Separation*, at the big picture. He thought that if he succeeded, "Spike Lee and [Steven] Spielberg and the big boys will want to work with me."

In an interview he gave just after filming had

begun, Will talked about the difficulty of his role and the demands of acting in general. "I had enough innate charm for the audience to make them buy that this guy could put one over on people. But the gay part . . . was really hard. I don't have anything against homosexuals—I'm just not one. So there was nothing I'd learned as an actor or done in my life that I could draw on."

The biggest obstacle for Will came when the script called on him to kiss fellow actor Anthony Michael Hall. Will could not do it. He recalled, "The director said, 'Don't worry, you're an actor, just get through it.' I said, 'You're going to have to work something else out.' It was my one real failure in that role, that I wasn't mature enough as an actor to accept the fact that I was acting."

Despite the setback, the film garnered critical praise not only for Stockard Channing and Donald Sutherland, who played the leading roles, but for Will as well. It was the break that Will needed. He has always acknowledged the experience of working on *Six Degrees of Separation* as the most important influence on the development of his acting career.

Will was soon back in front of the cameras shooting the 1995 action film *Bad Boys*, in which he costarred with another popular African-American comedian, Martin Lawrence. The film, which followed the exploits of two Miami policemen in their efforts to protect a witness, gave Will another opportunity to show his range and diverse talents. Although *Bad Boys* did not receive great reviews, Will's performance did. The movie was also a popular and financial success, which demonstrated that audiences would pay to see Will Smith in the movies. Will soon found himself in demand, and more scripts and offers started to come his way.

By 1995, Will felt the time was approaching to leave *The Fresh Prince of Bel Air*. For a year or more he had grown increasingly dissatisfied with the direction the show was taking. Although the program still received high ratings, Will thought the plots were becoming too frivolous and trivial. He wished the show could address more serious issues. At the end of the fifth season, therefore, Will gave notice that the next season would be his last. "I just felt it was time," he later explained. Acting in a television series "was a discipline I needed to learn and I did. I will miss the characters and doing the show, but it was just time. Besides I wanted to go out while the show was still hot. I never wanted to go out like a sucker, with them pushing me out."

After six successful seasons, the final episode of *The Fresh Prince of Bel Air* aired on May 20, 1996. Will had decided his acting was taking him in another direction.

Will also believed that he had outgrown his character. "My everyday life is now drastically different from that of the *Fresh Prince*," Will said. "It's become increasingly difficult to find that guy inside me." As much as he had enjoyed doing the series and as much as he had learned from it, he now saw his character was confining, and he was eager to see how far his talent would take him.

Around this time, Will was approached about appearing in a film to be called *Independence Day*. The film, which combined the elements of the science fiction, fantasy, adventure, and disaster genres, revolved around an alien invasion of the Earth. There were four main characters: the president of the United States, an underachieving computer wizard, a drunken Vietnam veteran who claims to have been abducted by aliens, and an ambitious marine fighter pilot who wants to be an astronaut. The plot, of course, turned on their efforts to defeat the alien invasion forces and to save the world.

From the beginning, the executive producer of the film, Dean Devlin, and screenwriter Roland Emmerich wanted Will Smith for the part of the fighter pilot, Captain Steven Hiller. Both had seen *Six Degrees of Separation* and were impressed with Will's talent. As Emmerich explained, Will had "this all-American quality about him. He's a guy's guy, but he's so charming and sure of himself that women like him." Devlin stated that he thought Will's character was "clearly the heart of the movie. [Steven Hiller] was the Everyman in America, the good GI Joe, like you would have seen in the old World War II movies." Will was thrilled, and eagerly accepted the role.

The opportunity to appear in *Independence Day* in the role of Steven Hiller came at a good time for Will. Between preparing for the film and getting ready to start the last season of *Fresh Prince*, Will was too busy to think about problems in his personal life.

In 1991, Will had met Sheree Zampino, a fashion design student, on the set of another hit NBC comedy, *A Different World*. While Sheree was less than impressed with Will, he continued to pursue her. His efforts eventually succeeded. A year after they had met, Will and Sheree were married and welcomed the arrival of their first child, a son, whom they named Will Smith III, but called Trey. At first, the couple seemed quite happy, but the strain caused by Will's career and workaholic drive took its toll. Will and Sheree struggled to make their marriage work, but by 1994, it was clear that it was not meant to be. For Will, the hardest part of the divorce was not the huge financial settlement he had to pay, but surrendering primary custody of Trey.

Having experienced his parents' divorce, Will knew that the end of a marriage was not the end of the world. Life would go on. But he worried how the split would affect his son, whom he loved deeply. Looking back at that time in his life, Will later remarked, "You know how you're on the freeway and you see that one car on the side of the road? Thousands of cars drive by it. Well, every once in a while it's your turn to be broken down. And you wait for the tow truck to come. That's how I viewed that difficult time in my life."

Will found an escape in preparing for his role as Steven Hiller. He learned basic flying skills by practicing in a flight simulator with an actual marine pilot. He also drilled with soldiers and worked with a personal trainer to build up his strength and conditioning. Despite the long hours, hard work, and his difficult personal situation, Will still joked on the set, often sending costar Jeff Goldblum into fits of laughter.

Once again Will's efforts paid dividends at the box office. *Independence Day* was the smash summer hit of 1996, and the highest-grossing film of the year. Will's portrayal of the sarcastic, cigar-chomping Steven Hiller was a big hit with audiences everywhere. In the first six days of the film's release, it grossed a record $96 million. Will Smith was now box-office gold and on his way to "saving the world every summer." Will knew he had hit the big time when, after the release of *Independence Day*, he received a call from one of the most influential filmmakers in Hollywood: Steven Spielberg. It seemed that Mr. Spielberg was making a movie in which Will just had to accept a starring role.

6

LOOKING AHEAD

"You have to do this movie. We don't even want to talk about it," Steven Spielberg told Will. According to Smith, "You just can't tell Steven Spielberg no." The film was *Men in Black*. In addition to Spielberg's insistence that Will do the film, Will's enjoyment of science fiction swayed his decision. The $5 million he was to be paid to play the part of Agent J may also have influenced him.

In the film, the officials of a top-secret government agency that monitors alien activity on Earth recruit Will's character to work for them. Will and his costar, Tommy Lee Jones, find themselves in the middle of a deadly plot conceived by an alien terrorist. To prevent the world from certain destruction, the two agents must find the intergalactic troublemaker and put a stop to his evil scheme. Once again, Will was the hero out to save the planet.

Men in Black opened on July 4, 1997, in theaters across the country. Like *Independence Day* the year before, *Men in Black* enjoyed both popular and critical acclaim, taking in $51 million in the first week after its release. Will joked about his annual summer job saving the Earth from destruction by aliens: "Oh yeah. July fourth is Big Willie weekend now. But

---

Will starred with Tommy Lee Jones in the 1997 summer hit, *Men in Black*. He also wrote and performed the film's title song, which won a Grammy for Best Rap Single.

that's a good thing, to be linked to new movies. . . . It's really tempting to keep making those blockbusters, but I want to try other things and do different types of movies too."

Besides starring in *Men in Black*, Will wrote and performed the film's title song, as well as several others for the soundtrack, which won recognition as Best Soundtrack at the American Music Awards in January 1998. "Men in Black," which served as the film's opening song, immediately went to the top of the charts, earning Will his third Grammy for Best Rap single of 1997. The accompanying video won an MTV Video Award for Best Video for a Film. Even the dance that Will performed in the video made its way onto American dance floors.

Will's professional life could not have been better. His personal situation had also improved since the divorce. In 1996, Will had begun dating actress Jada Pinkett. The two had known each other since 1990, when Jada read for the part of Will's girlfriend on *The Fresh Prince of Bel Air*. She did not get the part, but had stayed in contact with Will. Then, not long after Will's divorce, the two began dating. A year later, on New Year's Eve 1997, they married. In July 1998, Will and Jada welcomed the arrival of their first son, Jaden Christopher Syre Smith. Of his wife, Will says, "Jada is the first person I've been with willing to accept that it's not always going to be great." In another interview, Will stated that Jada "makes everything okay, no matter how difficult it gets . . . she's just someone with whom I can talk about anything."

Clearly, Will Smith was now an A-list actor who could pick and choose his roles. To finish out 1998, Will took the lead role in *Enemy of the State*, in which his character tries to stop a

LOOKING AHEAD

On December 31, 1997, Will Smith married actress Jada Pinkett. The couple has two children: Jaden Christopher Syre Smith and Willow Camille Reign Smith, along with Will's son Trey from his previous marriage.

group of conspirators against the government. Will especially gravitated to the role because of his own belief in the existence of government cover-ups and conspiracies. The film was not the hit that *Independence Day* and *Men in Black* had been, but it made a respectable showing, demonstrating once again Will's draw at the box office.

Will's success in films had confirmed his tremendous appeal to both black and white, male and female, and young and old audiences. Now Will was hoping he could repeat the magic in his next film, *Wild Wild West*, a remake of the popular 1960s television show, which opened in July 1999. Although the film competed against *The Phantom Menace*, the long-awaited next installment in the *Star Wars* saga, Will was not worried. "I think *Star Wars* has kind of released the pressure from everyone. Everyone knows [what] the number one movie of the year is going to be. So the pressure is really gone, in that sense. Now it's just a battle for number 2."

Wild Wild West opened to poor reviews and was not the big box office hit that everyone had anticipated. Undaunted, Will moved onto his next project, a Robert Redford film titled *The Legend of Bagger Vance*, in which he played the title role. A mysterious caddie, Bagger Vance helps a former champion golfer, played by Matt Damon, rediscover his game and his zest for life. Will was drawn to the script for a number of reasons. The project gave him an opportunity to work with someone he greatly admired in director Redford, and at the same time it gave him a chance to pursue one of his great passions, playing golf.

The role also required something of Will that he was not used to providing: subtlety. In his previous films, Will played larger-than-life characters. In *Bagger Vance,* he needed to draw on a softer, more subdued approach to make his character believable. In one interview, Will admitted to being somewhat uncomfortable with this approach: "I like it loud and clear, but for that reason it was good to play a character who isn't big and funny and is a lot more subdued. . . . [It enabled me] to explore other aspects of myself and emote in a way that's different from any of my past work."

In *The Legend of Bagger Vance*, Will once

again won praise from film critics, who lauded his ability to bring the character to life. To Robert Redford, Will had successfully mastered the challenge of "[letting] go of being Will Smith" and becoming Bagger Vance. It was a wonderful complement to Will's acting ability.

Both professionally and personally, the present and the future look bright for Will Smith. Recently, he and Jada welcomed a new addition to their family: Willow Camille Reign Smith was born on October 31, 2000. Will continues to look for suitable movie scripts. He and Jada have also completed a script scheduled to begin filming sometime within the next year. A sequel to *Men in Black* is in the works, as is a film biography on one of Will's idols, Muhammed Ali, with Will playing the lead role. Will also had plans to go back on the road with a "Willennium Tour" to promote his latest solo album, which was released in 1999.

What is the secret of Will Smith's success? To Will, the answer seems obvious: "It's the ears! Americans have an ear fetish. Absolutely. Americans love people with big ears—Mickey Mouse, Goofy, Ross Perot. America loves ears." More seriously, many find Will's persona and humor engaging, entertaining, and attractive. He comes across on film as someone with whom people want to be friends. Despite a few missteps along the way, it has been Will's sense of values and his down-to-earth personality that, in real life, have helped him to stay on track.

As a successful African-American actor, Will realizes that he has a difficult responsibility to assume. "It's uncomfortable sometimes because there are so few [African-American actors] in comparison to successful Caucasian actors. So few that every move you make is 'a step for your

Will's movie career has taken off with a string of blockbuster hits. Here Will is pictured with Muhammed Ali, whom he will portray in a new movie about the boxer's life and career.

people.' It's like 'Wow, that's a bit too much.' My only litmus test is 'Will my mother be embarrassed by the work I do?' As long as . . . my family [isn't] embarrassed, then it generally works out: for my people also."

Will plans on making the most of the opportunities that are sure to come his way. He admits to feeling so good these days that "it's almost a . . . shame. I just love my life, and I'm not one tiny bit ashamed to say so." What a life it has been so far: a hip-hop star at 18; bankrupt at 19, married and a father by 24; and divorced at 27. And at the ripe old age of 32, Will Smith looks forward to his ever-expanding repertoire of roles as a singer, actor, and box-office star. The only difference now is that he has learned to balance those demanding roles with those he enjoys even more: son, brother, husband, and father.

CHRONOLOGY

1968	Will Smith is born on September 25 in Philadelphia, Pennsylvania
1981	Parents divorce
1986	Forms rap duo of DJ Jazzy Jeff and Fresh Prince with Jeff Townes and releases first single, "Girls Ain't Nothing But Trouble"; graduates from Overbrook High School; makes first film appearance in *The Imagemaker*
1987	*Rock the House* is released
1988	*He's the DJ, I'm the Rapper* is released and goes triple platinum
1989	*And in This Corner* is released
1990	*The Fresh Prince of Bel Air* premieres on September 10
1991	*Homebase* is released
1992	Appears in the film *Where the Day Takes You*; marries Sheree Zampino; son Willard C. "Trey" Smith III is born
1993	*Code Red* released; Appears in *Made in America*; appears in *Six Degrees of Separation*
1995	Appears in *Bad Boys*; divorces Sheree Zampino
1996	The final episode of *The Fresh Prince of Bel Air* airs on May 20; stars in *Independence Day*
1997	Costars in the hit film *Men in Black*; releases first solo effort, *Big Willie Style*; marries Jada Pinkett
1998	Stars in *Enemy of the State*; son Jaden Christopher Syre Smith is born; single "Gettin' Jiggy Wit It" reaches number one on *Billboard* charts
1999	Costars in *Wild Wild West*; releases second solo album *Willennium*
2000	Costars in *The Legend of Bagger Vance*; daughter Willow Camille Reign Smith is born

ACCOMPLISHMENTS

Discography

1986   D.J. Jazzy Jeff and Fresh Prince

1987   *Rock the House*

1988   *He's the DJ, I'm the Rapper*

1989   *And in This Corner . . .*

1991   *Homebase*

1993   *Code Red*

1998   *Greatest Hits*

Solo Albums

1997   *Big Willie Style*

1999   *Willennium*

Awards

1988   American Music Award Best Rap Single "He's the DJ, I'm the Rapper"; Grammy Award Best Rap Performance

1989   American Music Awards for Best Rap Album and Best Rap Artist, while single "Parents Just Don't Understand" wins Grammy Award for Best Rap Single

1991   American Music Award Best Rap Single "Summertime"; Grammy Award Best Rap Performance by a Duo or Group; wins Nickleodeon Kid's Choice Award as Favorite TV actor

1992   NAACP Image Award Best Comedy Series *The Fresh Prince of Bel Air*; Image Award Outstanding Rap Artist

1995   NATO/ShoWest Award Male Star of Tomorrow

1996   Blockbuster Entertainment Award Best Male Newcomer in Action/Comedy *Bad Boys*

1997   Blockbuster Entertainment Award Favorite Actor—Sci-Fi *Independence Day*; NATO/ShoWest Award International Box Office Achievement; MTV Music Award for Best Video from a Film

1998 MTV Video Music Award Best Male Video "Just the Two of Us"; MTV Video Music Award Best Rap Video "Gettin' Jiggy Wit It"; Blockbuster Entertainment Award Favorite Actor—Sci-Fi *Men in Black*; MTV Movie Award Best Movie Song "Men in Black"; 25th Annual American Music Award Favorite Soundtrack *Men in Black*; Grammy Award Best Rap Solo Performance "Men in Black"

1999 MTV Europe Music Award Best Male Performer; MTV Video Music Award Best Male Video "Miami"; ShoWest Convention Actor of the Year; Image Award special award—Entertainer of the Year; Grammy Award Best Rap Solo Performance "Gettin' Jiggy Wit It"; Image Award Outstanding Music Video "Just the Two of Us"; Image Award Outstanding Rap Artist "Just the Two of Us"; 20th Annual *Billboard* Music Video Best Pop Clip of the Year "Just the Two of Us"; American Music Award Pop/Rock Favorite Album *Big Willie Style*; American Music Award Soul/R&B Favorite Album *Big Willie Style*; American Music Award Soul/R&B Favorite Male Artist; Grammy Award Best Rap Solo Performance "Gettin' Jiggy Wit It"

2000 NAACP Image Award Outstanding Rap Artist, *Wild Wild West*; NAACP Image Award Outstanding Music Video, *Wild Wild West*; American Music Award Best Male Artist; American Music Award Best Soundtrack, *Wild Wild West*

Television

1990 *The Fresh Prince of Bel Air*

1991 *Blossom* (Cameo appearance as himself)

Films

1986 *The Imagemaker*

1992 *Where the Day Takes You*

1993 *Made in America*
     Six Degrees of Separation

1995 *Bad Boys*

1996 *Independence Day*

1997 *Men in Black*

1998 *Enemy of the State*

1999 *Wild Wild West*

2000 *The Legend of Bagger Vance*

Further Reading

Berenson, Jan. *Will Power! A Biography of Will Smith.* New York: Pocket Books, 1997.

Marron, Maggie. *Will Smith: From Rap Star to Mega-Star.* New York: Warner Books, 2000.

Nickson, Chris. *Will Smith.* New York: St. Martin's Press, 1999.

Robb, Brian J. *Will Smith: King of Cool.* New York: Plexus, 2000.

Stern, Dave. *Will Smith.* New York: Simon and Schuster, 1999.

About the Author

MEG GREENE earned a bachelor's degree in history at Lindenwood College in St. Charles, Missouri, and master's degrees in history and historic preservation from the University of Nebraska at Omaha and the University of Vermont, respectively. Ms. Greene is the author of nine other books, writes regularly for *Cobblestone* magazine and other publications, and serves as a contributing editor for Suite 101.com's "History For Children." She makes her home in Midlothian, Virginia.

INDEX

Ali, Tatyana, 40-41
And in This Corner (album), 33, 36
Arsenio Hall Show (TV), 37
Bad Boys, 48
Big Willie Style (album), 7-10, 57
Bright, Helen (grandmother), 9, 17-18, 24-25, 33
Channing, Stockard, 48
Civil rights movement, 13-14
Code Red (album), 45-46
Columbia Records, 9
Damon, Matt, 56
Danson, Ted, 45
Devlin, Dean, 50
Emmerich, Roland, 50
Enemy of the State, 54-55
Fresh Prince of Bel Air, The (TV), 39-41, 42, 43, 45, 49, 50, 54
"Gettin' Jiggy Wit It" (song), 8
"Girls Ain't Nothing But Trouble" (song), 30
Goldberg, Whoopi, 45
Goldblum, Jeff, 51
Goodman, Dana, 26, 29-30
Hall, Anthony Michael, 48
He's the DJ, I'm the Rapper (album), 31-32

Holmes, Clarence "Clate," 25-26, 28
Homebase (album), 41-42, 45
Imagemaker, The, 45
Independence Day, 9, 49-50, 51, 53, 55
Internal Revenue Service, 35
Jive Records, 30, 31, 32
Jones, Quincy, 38, 39
Jones, Tommy Lee, 53
"Just the Two of Us" (song), 10
Lawrence, Martin, 48
Lee, Spike, 47
Legend of Bagger Vance, The, 56-57
LL Cool J, 31
Made in America, 45
Medina, Benny, 38-39
Men in Black, 53-54, 55, 57
"Men in Black" (song), 54
Murphy, Eddie, 39
NBC network, 39, 41
"Nightmare on My Street" (song), 32
"Parents Just Don't Understand" (song), 31-32, 33
Philadelphia, Pennsylvania, 11, 13, 20, 24, 27, 30, 39
Pinkett, Jada (second wife), 8, 10, 54, 57
Public Enemy, 30, 31

Redford, Robert, 56
Rock the House (album), 30
Six Degrees of Separation, 46-48, 50
Smith, Caroline (mother), 14, 15, 17, 18-20, 21, 25, 26, 30-31, 32, 36, 51, 58
Smith, Ellen (sister), 14, 19
Smith, Harry (brother), 14, 19, 21
Smith, Jaden Christopher Syre (son), 54
Smith, Pamela (sister), 14, 19
Smith, Willard, Sr. (father), 14, 15, 16-17, 18-20, 21, 25, 26, 28-29, 30-31, 36, 51
Smith, Willard "Will" C., Jr.
  albums, 7-10, 30, 31-33, 36, 41-42, 45-46, 57
  awards, 7-8, 11, 33, 42, 54
  bankruptcy, 35-37, 45, 58
  birth, 14
  childhood, 15-29
  divorce, 51, 54, 58
  education, 18, 21, 25, 26, 28, 29
  and films, 9, 11, 45, 46-50, 51, 53-57

   as Fresh Prince, 10,
      11, 29-41, 47, 49,
      50, 54
   marriages, 50, 54, 58
   and rap music, 7-11,
      15, 21, 23-33, 41-42,
      45-46, 57, 58
   and television, 10, 11,
      37-41, 42, 43, 45,
      49, 50, 54

Smith, Will III "Trey"
   (son), 8, 10, 50-51
Smith, Willow Camille
   Reign (daughter), 57
Spielberg, Steven, 47,
   51, 53
Sutherland, Donald, 48
Townes, Jeff "DJ Jazzy
   Jeff," 10, 26-28, 29-33,
   35, 41-42, 43, 45-46

Warner Brothers
   Records, 38
*Where the Day Takes
   You*, 45
Wild, Wild, West, 56
Word Up, 26
Zampino, Sheree
   (first wife), 50

PHOTO CREDITS:

2:   Dennis Van Tine/ London Features Int'l
6:   Fitzroy Barrett/Globe Photos
11: Ron Wolfson/London Features Int'l
12: Bruce Cotler/Globe Photos
16: Tom Rodriguez/ Globe Photos
19: © Judy Hasday
20: Ralph Dominguez/ Globe Photos
22: Ron Wolfson/London Features Int'l
27: Ron Wolfson/London Features Int'l
31: Ralph Dominguez/ Globe Photos
34: Photofest
37: Gregg DeGuire/ London Features Int'l
40: Sylvia Sutton/Globe Photos
43: Neal Preston/Corbis
44: Photofest
47: Photofest
49: Lisa Rose/Globe Photos
52: Photofest
55: AP/Wide World Photos
58: AP/Wide World Photos

Cover photo: Ron Wolfson/London Features Int'l